PRESCRIPTION *for* SURVIVAL

Number Ten
Bampton Lectures in America
Delivered at Columbia University 1957

PRESCRIPTION

for SURVIVAL

by BROCK CHISHOLM

NEW YORK 1957

COLUMBIA UNIVERSITY PRESS

CONTENTS

PRESCRIPTION *for* SURVIVAL

THE PROSPECT
BEFORE US

No SANE man would refuse the gift of robust, glowing health—if such a gift could somehow suddenly be conferred upon him, if he could somehow be assured of a lifetime guarantee, not only against the more serious or fatal diseases, but also against the minor aches and pains, the common colds and digestive calamities that plague our daily living. No sane man would say that the state of his physical well-being was a matter of complete indifference to him. But unfortunately, too many of us tend to consider our health only in these limited, physical terms, in a completely negative sense, as merely the absence of disease or infirmity.

When I say that I am going to discuss health, I am not going to limit myself to these matters at all. I certainly am not going to dole out advice about seeing one's doctor, seeing one's dentist—or even about seeing one's psychiatrist. The health of a human being today must take in his ability to function wholly, to function wholly in all circumstances —physical, mental, and social. The truly healthy human being can use his physical equipment to the full extent of its capacity, his mental equipment to the full reaches of its potentiality, and his social equipment in a way that makes him a valuable member of the human race.

This concept of health will leave me free to wander very widely indeed. It will give me plenty of room in which to maneuver and give me license to talk about almost anything I wish.

My subject may be unlimited, but my time and space are not. And in setting forth one's thoughts and ideas in a relatively short space, it necessarily follows, I suppose, that one must generalize. And when one generalizes, it further follows that many of the things one says may not be true in a strictly scientific sense. I hope the reader will take for granted the kinds of reservations and exceptions, the extensions that I would make were this to be a more lengthy discussion. Certain somewhat broad statements will seem open to challenge, question, or counterstatement, but they must remain broad. There is no time to refine them to a point of universal acceptance.

The lack of time seems to be a malady of our age. Yet for a long time—at least for a long time as human time goes— the human race has been doing very well for itself. It has been competing successfully with all other forms of life. Quite a long time ago the human race learned to defend itself with sufficient skill to offset any great challenge to its existence and its continued development from large animals or medium-sized animals, and now gradually even the very small ones are being brought under control.

The time has now come when there is no threat to man from any competition on this little earth—that is, to man as a race. To individual men, still, yes, but in almost every case those forms of life which still are capable of damaging man are controllable. They are controllable whenever man is willing to invest enough time and energy to win dominion over the forms of life that still plague him. The one or two possible exceptions that still exist almost certainly will be controllable within the very near future. Even the filterable viruses, man's last competitors, are now being brought under his jurisdiction.

Man has been able to effect this disastrous (disastrous, that is, for some other forms of life but very beneficial for himself) competition by the use of his unique equipment. He is not able to compete on the same ground as many other forms of life: his teeth are not very good for either offensive or defensive purposes; his claws are ludicrously inadequate—although some people do tend to use them still; he can't run very fast, jump very high, or swim very well; his eyes can't compare with those of certain other animals. In fact, compared with other forms of life, he is not very "good at" most activities.

There is one thing, however, that man has, one thing that is far better than in any other form of life—the superior lobes of his brain. As far as is known or can be known at this time, this is man's unique equipment (and then, only in degree) that is better than that of any other form of life. Man's method of competing is *thinking*. This is what he is equipped to be "good at."

This does not necessarily mean that he uses his equipment as well as it might be used. We may even suspect that most people don't think well at all. In fact, it appears that we, people generally, have been trained from infancy not to be able to think. And if, as a result of changing circumstances some time later in life, it appears desirable to begin to think, we find that process extremely difficult and painful. Most of us creak very badly indeed, when we try to use these unused thinking muscles of ours.

Actually, these superior lobes that we have are tremendously efficient. We have an enormous capacity for thinking that very few people in the world really use effectively. It may be that only by more efficient use of his thinking equipment may man learn how to survive—if he is going to survive—under new circumstances in a changed world.

It would seem that man is in a precarious position now, but not a position at all unique, because many forms of life have been in this position before—shortly before they disappeared—when their environment had changed so greatly that they were not able to make an adequate adjustment to the great change. Every form of life is always in a test situation, a test of whether it is able to make adequate adjustment to changing circumstances. When any form of life at any time is not able to make that kind of adjustment, it disappears.

Even in our own lifetime, we find a number of forms of life that have not been able to compete because of changed circumstances, and have disappeared, or almost disappeared. The buffalo (the bison of the western plains), the passenger pigeon, the whooping crane, and many other kinds of birds and animals have been or are now in the process of disappearing, unless man can take effective steps to keep them alive. Competitively they have lost out. They are not able to keep going by their own actions.

If we look back into world history we find that this has happened many times before. The brontosaurus, the icthyosaurus, a lot of big fellows and a great many little ones, have disappeared—in many cases, after having lived and flourished for far longer than man has. I think it is essential for us to remind ourselves that man has no permanent mortgage on this little earth. He may survive if he is able to survive and, just as true, he may not survive if he is not able to make adequate adjustment to a changing environment.

In recent years man's circumstances have indeed changed, and changed drastically, changed perhaps just as much as, and perhaps more than, the alterations that were induced by the great ice ages which destroyed so many forms of life. The most important change of recent years is that man's ability to kill has reached a universal level.

This is not to say that the nature of man himself has changed. Man has always been an enthusiastic killer. He has always tried to kill other men, as well as other forms of life, but until quite recently he did it in a retail sort of way, one at a time and not very efficiently. And just as we have improved the efficiency of many things our ancestors did, we have enormously increased our efficiency in killing.

For many years there was a very comforting old saying that was taught to every staff officer in all armies when he was taking his training. This saying was never true, but it was comforting. It was to the effect that the defense always overtakes the offense. Whenever the enemy (that is, the "bad ones," the enemy) had bigger and better guns than we (the "good ones") had, we could comfort ourselves by saying that some defensive weapon would be invented to counteract them, that offense is always overtaken by defense. Actually, what happened was that improved offense rendered all previous offense obsolete. Defense never overtook offense, but more potent offense came into style.

That was valid; it worked. We were able to measure strength in terms of armament, manpower, and all sorts of things that do not apply any more, because now that the power to kill has become universal, it doesn't matter very much whether people are going to be killed by hydrogen bombs or some other kind of bombs or by biologicals, or whatnot. Once it is possible to destroy whole populations, it doesn't matter very much how you do it. We can no longer even pretend that defense can overtake offense. In fact, it has become perfectly clear that the whole business of warfare is obsolete as a human behavior pattern.

But it would appear that we still have the aggressive pressures, the hostilities, the kinds of feelings that all through human history have led to warfare, led to fighting each other, led to the killing of as many people as possible by the "good ones" and the "bad ones" both. However, we are in a situation totally unexpected to any of our ancestors; none of our ancestors had any idea that genocide could happen. (The term even appears only in the "New Words" section of Webster's Unabridged Dictionary!) But because it can happen, and because the patterns of our ancestors invariably led to fighting wars, we who are now at this stage of human development must begin to recognize that our generation has a responsibility that no generation of the human race has ever had before. Never before has man himself been the enemy of mankind. Never before could man destroy the human race, or distort it genetically to the point where its evolution would change drastically. Never before has any generation held a veto power over the continuing evolution of human beings.

That is the situation now. It is a situation for which we, the people of the world, have not been prepared, historically, educationally, or morally, because this situation did not enter into the moral concept, the educational concept, or any other concept of our ancestors, even our immediate ancestors, even our own parents.

We must recognize that the attitudes they expressed, the attitudes instilled in ourselves at very deep levels as conscience values, may have been appropriate in past generations, but they may not be appropriate now. We must recognize that we do not know that anything of the attitudes of our ancestors can still be accepted without question, because we do know that their behavior led to killing which would now become universal if it were repeated, if that pattern continued only a little longer.

It would seem that our responsibility, then, is to re-examine all of the attitudes of our ancestors and to select from those attitudes things which we, on our own authority in these present circumstances, with our knowledge, recognize as still valid in this new kind of world. This is not to say that we should discard everything of the past any more than that we should accept everything of the past. But it is to say that we are the authority—that we can no longer lean on our ancestors for authoritative attitudes. We must trust ourselves to do our own thinking and make sure it is relevant to this real situation of the present time.

The human race today is worried. There seems to be a

large body of, one might say, "free-floating" anxiety that is a part of everyone's life. It is not necessarily seen to belong to its real source, but maybe just felt as a discomfort and unhappiness, a fear that "something is wrong." Without consciously thinking about it, one may be worried, not sleep very well, have certain vague symptoms, nervousness, bad dreams. This anxiety seems to be pervasive; it is showing up in many fields that only a few years ago were relatively serene.

It is a valid anxiety. There is, for the first time in human history, a valid anxiety for the whole human race. We are right to be worried. We have true, real cause for being concerned, because we are living in dangerous times for all of us.

Whenever the human race, or, in fact, any form of life, finds itself in difficulties, there is a very common pattern of behavior. One normally tries one's most mature behavior, and if it works, very well. If it doesn't work effectively for one's own security, then there is a tendency to back up, to regress, to move backward to an older, well-tried form of behavior which was effective at a somewhat lower level of development.

All children do this when they find themselves in difficulty. A six-year-old child finding himself in trouble, frightened, may try his six-year-old behavior, but he's not very confident about that, and having tried it, perhaps only very briefly, he tends, if the situation still is threatening, to back up to five-year-old or four-year-old or even earlier behavior.

But not only children act in this way; so does everyone else. Because this new situation for which we have no training is pervasive on such a great scale, because there are so many things involved about which we feel anxious, about which we feel we can do little or nothing individually, very many of us in many parts of the world are tending to regress. Because we have not found any rational way of behaving effectively to escape or to change the circumstances so that we will no longer have to feel anxious, we must expect that we, the people of the world, in large numbers, will have an urge to behave in less mature ways than we are capable of were we not so deeply anxious. There are many, many examples of this, many symptoms of this type of regression.

We find it in people who, at their best, at their most mature, should and would know better. We find people who have been relatively mature in their attitudes, who have made great achievements in science and culture, submitting to the wills of dictators, consciously and intentionally so submitting. This is, of course, regressive. It is an attempt to avoid responsibility for oneself, to go back to the stern father image for security, to find the big, strong person who will take the responsibility, so that one won't have to do any worrying oneself.

In other parts of the world, instead of submitting to a self-appointed dictator, people are electing a benevolent father image, a gentle strong man, a great person who is going to take all the responsibility and fix everything so that, again, we don't have to do any worrying. This is called "hero worship," a very common and juvenile attitude that is commonly substituted for taking personal responsibility for what happens.

There are other people who achieve escape by going backwards socially, by believing not in an individual, but in a social structure, which presents final decisions, so that the individual need not decide things for himself. Many people who are anxious yearn for such a social structure. They believe that if they, under the aegis of society, have only to do as they are told, be obedient—in effect, be good little boys and girls—they will be looked after and protected, and everything will be all right.

Other people show a touching faith in the value of organization. Organization has become a great cure-all in the minds of many. To set up an organization, they say, is to have accomplished something.

This, too, is regressive. It is regressive to the extent that people believe that an organization will by itself do something constructive and relieve them of anxiety, that it will make arrangements, for instance, that nobody will fight anybody else, that everybody will be fed, that nobody will be allowed to encroach on our ground, and that everybody will be made nice and happy and prosperous without any great cost to ourselves—certainly with no reduction in our standard of living or in any less space and raw materials for ourselves.

These are manifestly incompatible requirements for any person who thinks about it, and yet these hopes have been expressed merely as the result of setting up an organization. Many people have thought, "Now we can go home and just enjoy ourselves, and only worry whether we are going to get a pink and purple car, or have to get along with the green and yellow one we had last year," just because we have set up an organization to carry our responsibilities for us. Hardly anything could be more ridiculous. A mere organization isn't going to solve all the problems of mankind. It never has, and it never will.

Surely it is clear to people who are able to think at all that none of the world's problems is going to be settled inside any one culture. We must not think in terms that include the idea that the welfare of any one group is more important than that of any other group—which still remains the original premise of unthinking people in the world today. It is quite clear that major problems are going to be decided and settled only by the peoples of the world, whenever they grow up enough and are able to behave maturely enough to be able to cope with those problems.

Consider, for instance, the population problem. We, the peoples of the world, are now increasing at a rate of about 32,000,000 or so a year—about 85,000 a day is our net increase. This is so frightening that we tend to look away from it and not let ourselves think about it at all. Because I happen to be a Canadian, I tend to think of it in terms of twice the population of Canada being added to the world's population each year.

It is also a fact that we are not increasing our ability to feed people at anything like that rate. It is not just a question of growing food. We probably could, if we worked hard at it, but we're not doing so, because we are not able to distribute properly even the food we grow and produce now, because we don't know how.

We have consistently avoided the real, basic problems of population increase and food supply and distribution, just as we have avoided the implications of the natural resources situation. For instance, at the present time North America is using just about half of the total production of irreplaceable natural resources of the world. Since the First World War—which wasn't so very long ago—North America has used up as much of these irreplaceable natural resources as the whole human race had used up to that time.

This is a serious condition. How much longer is North America going to be allowed to use half the production of the natural resources of the world? One might guess, possibly ten years—perhaps not so long. It may be that we should be doing a great many things about this situation that we have hardly begun to think about. A few people are making preparations. Some have their eyes on the African and Antarctic continents, and are beginning to say, "Oh, we could get plenty of stuff from Africa and Antarctica." It may be. There may be extensive resources in those continents, but who is going to get them?

Well, it's perfectly clear who should get them, isn't it? The peoples of Africa and Asia, because they are the ones who need them. They need them far more than anybody in North America needs them, and surely we can't take for granted that this absurd pattern of a very few people in the world using up such a completely out-of-proportion share of natural resources will be allowed to continue much longer until the last great reservoir of such resources is used up. That wouldn't make sense to anybody, unless he happened to be a North American.

Never in human history has the distribution of great reservoirs of natural resources been decided except by bloody warfare and wholesale death. Perhaps the next and greatest challenge to the will and the ability of the human race to survive will be when the time comes to apportion the riches of the African and Antarctic continents. It is time that we begin to think about that as one of the major problems facing us.

We must abandon any idea that our first obligation is to maintain our own standard of living. As long as we believe that our standard of living is more important than the very lives of hundreds of millions of other people, we cannot expect to be regarded with any great degree of admiration or respect.

The inhabitants of North America already have a standard of living completely out of reach of most people in the world, and it is senseless for us to say that our goal is to raise the standard of living of countries like India to approximate our own. India doesn't even have room enough for her present population, let alone for her increase of five or so million a year (which is not as great an increase per capita as that in North America). Certainly there is no room for the things we regard as essential to our standard of living: thousands of miles of four- and six-lane highways; clover leafs that take up twenty acres or more of good arable land; golf courses; sports arenas—all these things consume enormous quantities of good land.

We have hardly begun to face up yet to what we are doing. To give a minor example: every year we are using up several hundred, or perhaps several thousand, new acres, usually of perfectly good land, just to bury people in after they are dead! Can anyone imagine a more purposeless use of land? And it reduces our capacity to grow food. If

India tried to use, proportionate to her population, the same amount of land that we do for cemeteries, she simply wouldn't have the room, and the pitiful amount of food she is able to grow to feed her present population would be even more inadequate.

Before we speak glibly about other people's standards of living being raised to approximate ours, let us first face the facts of life, the realities of what we are talking about. It could be done. It could be done if we were willing to reduce our standard of living to meet theirs somewhere on a lower level, but so far we have shown no signs whatever of being willing to go so far as that, even in the interests of security.

However, the real necessity is not nearly so much an actual lowering of our standard of living as it is an expression of willingness not to concern ourselves so much about our standard of living. What is clear is that something must be done about the distribution of food on a world basis. I cannot see any prospect of real peace and security until that can be arranged.

This does suggest the desirability, the inevitability, the necessity of very extensive changes in our economic system, because our economic systems were all designed for ruthless competition, not for the kind of necessities we have prescribed in the Charter of the United Nations as a minimum requirement for the survival of the human race.

In our relations with peoples in other parts of the world our high standard of living is undoubtedly a great handicap, because it inevitably produces a high level of jealousy. If we could in some way find measures of indicating that some of us, at least, think we don't have to go on raising our standard of living, that we could wait until other people in the world catch up a little bit—if we could find a way of indicating that—we would have taken a tremendous step forward in the eyes of other people. We would give proof of our interest in world peace and world security.

But it is much easier for us to disregard this jealousy, to be complacent, to "pat ourselves on the back." After all, we are a hardworking, industrious people. Some of us have struggled to get our education. We take menial jobs during the day and go to school at night. Others of us get up at six o'clock in the morning and work hard all day to produce the goods which have made this country prosperous.

What if North America does have more than half the world's natural resources? Is the standard of living in China today any different than it was two thousand years ago? Isn't her standard of living and that of India a reflection of her culture, of her philosophical point of view toward life? And is it really an accident that our culture has evolved differently from other cultures of the world? Weren't all our scientific technological advances and so on rather a steady stream, one leading to the other? And couldn't other cultures have picked them up hundreds of years ago and followed us in a parallel pattern? After all, when we were mere colonies we were poor compared to other countries, but we have evolved with a steady, purposeful program. Aren't we to be admired for this rather than resented and envied?

Many of us have had disturbing experiences with students we have met here from other countries—students from India, China, or the Sudan. These students certainly do not represent the poorest classes of their country; many of them are here on scholarships provided by us and by our governments. Yet we are dismayed to hear them expressing hostile attitudes toward us. They say that they do not need a bomb to kill us; they will destroy us by superiority of numbers. They verbally shake their fists and say that the brown man or the yellow man must and will take his place in the world. All this bewilders us; we feel hurt, if not downright angry.

It is true that some students who come to our country try to make difficulties. But we must remember that when they come, they usually find themselves surrounded by people who discount every value of their culture, people who take for granted that everything in our country is superior to everything in their country. No foreign student can accept this, and he shouldn't, because it isn't true. They do admire the equipment and industry and so on, but at the same time they think that we in North America are far too concerned about stuff and things. They regard these as less important than what they think of as more spiritual values.

If we were to come from those cultures to this culture, our envy also would be overwhelming, and we undoubtedly would sooner or later express it in the very terms that they do—terms which represent a reaction that has been piling up for years and only rarely, if ever, expressed before. That reaction is quite understandable. These students have behind them a suffering people, ill and old and hopeless. They see wealth here, and waste, and are met with a lack of sympathy toward their own cultural values. Naturally and inevitably they feel antagonistic.

A man of Southeast Asia cannot get up at six o'clock in the morning and work hard all day. In his climate it is impossible. But it is also impossible because he hasn't the health and energy for it. When he doesn't have to work, and when he is not searching for food, he lies down, because he is tired and sick and starving. To help him control the diseases that plague him, to help him get enough food so that he is not hungry and so that he will have the energy and the will to work, as he does not now, will require unlimited patience.

The changing of these conditions is a growth process. It will be slow and will have to be done very carefully, small step by small step, if it is going to be effective. There is no easy path that can do anything constructive about this tremendously important and enormous problem that faces the world.

But there is still another new situation in the world, for which we have no preparation. Our organizations, our national constitutions, our methods of doing business, our monetary systems, all our institutions, were never designed to solve these problems at all. They were designed for quite different problems and for quite different circumstances, and none of them was developed for this kind of world. They were developed for a quite, quite different world, the world of our forebears. Yet we find ourselves now trying to implement new attitudes with instruments that are pretty obsolete—at least we would find them so if we bothered to really examine them. But we have a great loyalty to our institutions; we don't like to examine them for fear we would find that they need very drastic changing —which might conceivably be quite uncomfortable for ourselves. Up until now we have not expected ourselves to develop much beyond a national loyalty—which is a kind of institution. Indeed, very large numbers of us have not developed much beyond loyalty to family or to an arbitrarily defined group, a group defined by such criteria as color or religion or ideology or some geographical feature —which are other kinds of institutions.

But it is quite clear, now that the human race is threatened, that we must begin to learn to behave as thinking human beings—the behavior that our educational and moral systems have not been designed for; indeed, in many cases the behavior they have been designed to prevent. Generally they have set up circumscribed, limiting loyalties which now hinder us from functioning as members of the human race. It is in these areas that we must begin to function; and it is not easy, because we have to start with our own limitations, our own prejudices.

The thing we should not do is to refuse to think about anything uncomfortable or dangerous or threatening, to shut our eyes and hope that these problems will go away, all by themselves. One symbol of this attitude—which I hope you do not have in your home—is the three little monkeys, one with its hand over its ears, one with its hands over its eyes, and the third with its hands over its mouth, and the perfectly dreadful text that goes with it: "Hear no evil; see no evil; speak no evil."

I cannot imagine anything worse to believe or to teach a child than that. Because if there is an evil, what it needs most is to be heard, looked at, and talked about. Unless it is heard and seen and talked about, nothing will be done about it, and no evil has ever been exorcised by covering the ears or the eyes or the mouth.

The ostrich is supposed to behave like this, by hiding its head in the sand, but we all know that it doesn't really. The ostrich is a very sensible bird. It is man who tries to do the hiding, because he has been taught to, in most cases, in early childhood.

What I am really advocating is that we all should have a true scientific attitude or employ scientific method—and I use these words without holding them to the rigid definitions assigned to them by the physical scientists. Inevitably, when we are developing as fast as we are now, and in as many areas as we are now, there is a tremendous variety of experiment going on. A great deal of knowledge is being accumulated. But because of habits ingrained in us in childhood, it is easy for us to say, "We have discovered ultimate truth. This is it. Now we've got it."

I think the true scientist never says that, and, again, I do not mean a true scientist in the physical-scientist sense only. What I mean is that a person who really has a scientific attitude can only say, "This seems to be a tenable thesis at the moment. If we consult other people doing other kinds of work, perhaps we will revise our own attitudes. As we go on learning more, we will revise them, we hope, still further." It is fluidity of attitude that I believe we should be assuming now.

In the human relations field, it is not possible to be strictly "scientific" in the sense of being able to reproduce absolutely an experiment that someone else has conducted, or to conduct again the same experiment on the same person, because, always, the person has changed as a result of the first experiment. It is possible, however, to keep a scientific attitude—an attitude which largely depends on the ability to learn from experience, which allows one to change one's mind with new evidence, which prevents one from nailing one's flag to any certainty. The true scientist believes what he has found until he gets better evidence, and then he changes his belief.

I would like to discuss this word "belief," if I may. Too many of us have confused our thinking, or have had our thinking confused for us, by the careless use of words, and two words that are frequently interchanged are "belief" and "faith." Faith is an absolute word, a flag nailed to a mast, not changeable except at the cost of acquiring a load of guilt or sin or anxiety. Belief is changeable, with changed evidence, with new experimentation, with new experience.

Most of us have been brought up to believe that faith—just faith in itself—is a good thing, and this is a teaching that we might well question. It is true that modern man, with the brainpower that he has now, does not have an effective capacity for faith that primitive man had. Man's brain now is more organized for the reception of evidence. It is developed, as are his nervous system and his senses, to take in new material, to sort it out, and to make him able to change his mind when he gets new evidence that makes something he believed before apparently less true than he had thought it to be. Can we think that faith—faith that blindly accepts, independent of evidence for or against—is man's highest form of development?

We know more now than any of our ancestors knew at any previous time. We have experience and evidence available in every field of human thinking and activity that goes far beyond any such knowledge available to any of our ancestors. This is not to say that our present knowledge is a finished product. But it does represent the thinking of the moment, it is in touch with reality, it is based on the most valid interpretation, wherever that is available, and it has not been nailed down and fixed, so that it remains changeable with changing or increasing evidence.

It is only through exercise of the scientific attitude that new knowledge can be gained. I believe that what hope there is lies in the realm of scientific attitude as I have defined it.

Perhaps our greatest responsibility is to help our children to grow beyond ourselves. It has been said that the worst thing that could happen to the next generation is that they might turn out to be just like us. That is true, because we are still the kind of people who have fought each other throughout human history, and we cannot afford to go on being that kind of people any longer. We need to begin to concern ourselves about how we can arrange to free our children from our prejudices, our limiting loyalties, so that they can go on from where we left off, and develop levels of maturity that are entirely beyond our possibilities.

But this responsibility must not become an excuse for us, particularly for elderly people, to say, "Well, of course, nobody can expect me at my age to go changing my mind about things. Everybody knows that when you get as old as I am, you get to be pretty rigid in your thinking; the young people should do all this, but certainly not me."

This is another method of escape. Evidence of this attitude has even been written into the constitutions of some of the agencies of the United Nations. There is one place in the Constitution of the World Health Organization, to which I will refer later, where it says that the healthy development of children ("healthy" meaning physically, mentally, and socially) is of basic importance, that essential to such development is the ability to live harmoniously in a changing total environment.

Nobody says, "*We* ought to do that," but the children are expected to "live harmoniously in a changing total environment," when many of us who are full-grown adults can't live harmoniously even in our own families we have lived in all our lives! We recognize the necessities, but postpone them for a generation or so—hang it on the children. They have to live harmoniously, and then everything will be all right.

Maybe some of us ought to learn this lesson also, or enough so, at least, that we may have a reasonable hope that the human race will survive long enough for our children to become mature to a degree that we have not been able to reach.

TOMORROW'S CHILDREN

WE HAVE BEEN discussing certain unpleasant realities of the world in which we now live, the world in which we hope to help our children to be able to live. We are not capable of living harmoniously in a changing total environment, as the people of the world have declared, in the Constitution of the World Health Organization, that it is necessary for the next generation to do. And unless we can free our children far more effectively than we have freed ourselves, there is not much likelihood that our children will achieve much more than we have achieved in the field of human relations.

The responsibility suggested by these statements is enormous, and it lies heavily on those people capable of seeing it and accepting it. That should, of course, include all the people who attend a university. Perhaps it doesn't, because some so-called universities have not been teaching universal values at all but only teaching conformity to one way of life, one religious attitude, or one set of group certainties. Such institutions, of course, have no right to call themselves universities. Their teaching is not universal.

I think every university has an obligation to consider

whether its teaching is in fact universal. Does it open all possible channels of knowledge to its students? Does it teach things in true perspective to each other? Does it take the same attitudes about other cultures as it does about the one in which it happens to be working?

That is one area of responsibility. All teachers share in this responsibility, and perhaps most particularly the teachers of the junior grades in school, which are tremendously more important in character formation than are the years at the university. Still more important are the responsibilities resting on parents, because the years in which the child is in the charge of his parents are immeasurably more important as far as his future life is concerned than are his earlier years in school.

Only now, recently, is it becoming generally recognized —and still not entirely by any means—that the role of the parent in relation to the upbringing of a child is perhaps the most important thing that happens in our culture. Also, it is being recognized that much has been learned about the process of development during the first five or six years of life. Psychologists, cultural anthropologists, social scientists, and psychiatrists have learned quite a bit about how children develop from birth toward maturity. But very little of that knowledge is yet implemented. In a few great centers of population, a few up-to-date people, aware of the world's present situation, aware of all the attempts to learn, to explore, to experiment, are thinking about these problems and are trying to straighten them out and to present us with a reasonably true picture for our consideration.

To be sure, the knowledge we have in the fields of human

relations and child development is still crude; it is far from perfected. But it is usable and is far more worthy of our confidence than are the "certainties" that were inculcated in us in our childhood—"certainties" conditioned by the accident of birth and heredity. Whatever its present limitations, it is a great improvement over the old habit of copying the patterns of our ancestors simply because they were the patterns of our ancestors.

It should be obvious, then, that our responsibility now is to help our children learn things and learn in ways that were not available to us when we were children. If they are going to make the kind of world in which security can be found, they will have to develop free of many limitations that still bind us.

Many people, who themselves have developed away from the "certainties" inculcated in them in their childhood—religious and others—who no longer believe what they were taught when they were children, send their children back, by their own teaching or by that of others, to learn things in terms which they themselves have discarded.

This is very queer, but it happens frequently. Such people differentiate between good and true. Some attitude, some belief may no longer be considered "true" by the parents, but they earnestly think that their child should believe it because it is "good." This contortion that many parents go through discounts entirely all the development of any one generation. It forces each generation to start all over again and to have to go through the same long, slow, painful process of fighting for liberation from binding "certainties" that were imposed in childhood. If children are lucky, before they die they may get to the same level their parents reached, but they won't get much farther.

This is unfair to children. Surely one's children should be given the advantages of one's own development. Surely they should not be tied hand and foot all over again as their parents were tied to the absolute certainties of the past generation. Millions of children in the world are now being tied to the certainties of ten and twenty and thirty generations ago by this mechanism wherein each generation refuses to let its children continue from the point it itself reached.

By advocating that we should free our children of the "certainties" of their ancestors, I do not mean that we should abolish religion or religious teaching. One cannot deny that, throughout human history, religion has been a tremendously important part of people's lives. It has represented, episodically at least, an attempt to understand, a striving to find this harmonious living about which we now try to talk scientifically.

I am not suggesting that no one needs religion, or that we should become antireligious and get rid of it. Not only do many people need some kind of religion, they need different kinds of religion. They need different beliefs, and if they have that need, they should be free to seek whatever it is that they need.

What I am suggesting is that they should not be tied to the system of beliefs to which their parents happen to adhere, beliefs often acquired through the accident of birth into a particular family at a particular time in a particular place. Surely the time has come when the human race should learn to take charge of its own destiny, and no longer submit itself to the mercy of these accidents.

It is the teaching of unchangeable attitudes that makes trouble. The problem is not created nearly so much by the content of an orthodoxy as by the fact of an orthodoxy. It is not the teaching of an attitude—however it is taught —that is damaging, nearly so much as the teaching that it is fixed and final and that one is forbidden to think about it. This is damaging because children very early in their lives get the idea they should stop their thinking every time they run into anything uncomfortable or dangerous or threatening.

Children need to make their peace with religion—everybody does in some way, but it is hard to justify the parents who will prescribe one particular religion for their children in a way that can make them feel guilty, ashamed, and subject to a variety of neurotic difficulties if they dare to change their minds about it.

I believe that every child should be taught in his early years the facts of religion, the tremendous importance that religion has had in the lives of most of the people of the world; that he should be helped to understand what religion has done, what it has done for people and what it has done to them; how it has been used effectively and satisfactorily under some circumstances and disastrously under others.

The principles of all the great religions, the ethical attitudes, are much the same, giving or taking a little on account of the particular culture in which a particular religion developed, but the expression of them was the expression that was typical of the culture, and it could not be anything else. The child should be taught this.

One of the commonly shared religious codes is the Ten Commandments. As in many other schemes of ethics, there is very much truth and wisdom in them, but some of them, I think, are not as wise as others, shall we say? For instance, the injunction to honor thy father and mother that thy days may be long in the land was perfectly satisfactory in the kind of system in which it was said; that is, if you didn't honor your father and mother, they were entitled to do you in, because it was that kind of society.

But honoring fathers and mothers now does not necessarily lengthen one's days at all. I think it is much more satisfactory to see fathers and mothers clearly, and they will be honored if they are honorable, they will be respected if they merit respect, they will be loved if they are lovable. But commanding children to do that sort of thing is totally futile. It doesn't have any useful effect or value.

In fact, I do not believe the imposing of any commandments on children is effective. I believe that they need an object lesson before them, a picture of what man-and-woman behavior is like at its best, as seen in their fathers and mothers, and then they will grow into that picture more satisfactorily than will children who have commandments imposed upon them.

There are such things, of course, as matters of faith. This, I believe, the child needs to be told perfectly clearly; that something is a matter of faith with the parent, and then it should be explained why the parent believes in or has this particular faith. If it is the accident of his birth, the child should know it. If the parent has been convinced by someone's arguments, that too needs to be told to the child. But the important thing to remember is that just because the parent has adopted a faith, it is not necessarily at all the best faith for a child, or for a child when he grows up. That should be for him to decide, not the parent or anybody else.

Because the childhood of every person remains part of him all his life, it surely is reasonable to suggest that we should never teach anything to children that is not literally true, because children have very literal minds. We must realize that children and grownups are continuous. No person is one year old and then stops being one year old and becomes two years old. No person is five years old and stops being five years old and is ten years old, or stops being ten years old and is twenty or thirty or forty years old.

Every person is the accumulated sum of his whole experience. There is a one-year-old in every grownup extant, still there, with the attitudes the one-year-old child had. Every person extends from his infancy to his latest development, but he doesn't stop being one thing when he takes on something else. He adds his experience to his accumulated total; thus there is a part of every person that has the necessities of the infant, the necessities of the child also, the necessities of the juvenile, the young adult, and eventually added to it the necessities of the old person. Each part of this extended personality needs its particular types of satisfaction.

This concept is important. Many people feel that it doesn't matter very much what you teach a two-year-old child because he is going to stop being a two-year-old child and after a while be a five-year-old child, which is a different thing. It isn't. The two-year-old child is still the basis, the foundation, for the five-year-old child, and the five-year-old child is the first or second or fifth story of the building that will be the adult later on. If the five-year-old child is broken up in pieces, if he has conflicts within his personality, if parts of himself are at war with other parts of himself, it will be extremely difficult for him to act as a sound foundation for the grown-up person that he will later become. If continual building goes on, as it does in every intelligent person, on the foundation of childhood experience, by the time he has added thirty or forty or fifty stories, as it were, the stability of the early stories becomes tremendously important. It will determine whether the upper levels of his structure will stand or not, because the early stories are still part of the personality, indeed they are the very foundation of every personality.

This, I think, we have not learned sufficiently. When we think about it, we all know that it is true, and yet we feel that we have a license, as it were, to misinform children without any feeling of irresponsibility; to tell them weird things; even to teach them things or have other people teach them things that we don't believe ourselves.

This, of course, is unfair not only to the individual child, but is unfair socially, unfair to the human race, because the human race cannot afford to have good material spoiled, good material which might contribute to its eventual security.

These are responsibilities that lie firmly on parents. Nobody else can take their place. Later on teachers can help, but a teacher may spend all his time and effort in only trying to repair some of the damage done by parents without doing any really constructive thing, just repairing damage. If that is necessary—and it may take years to repair the damage if it can ever be done at all—much time is wasted, and the child will probably not be able to develop to anywhere near the degree of maturity that he should have been able to reach if his parents hadn't crippled him when he was very young.

Most of our children are exposed to lies regularly. Parents generally have two entirely separate standards of truth—one for children and one for everybody else. Of course there are parents who simply lie to everybody, but even for those who consider themselves "honest," lying to children seems to be entirely outside the moral code.

I remember being tremendously impressed with this phenomenon years ago, when I was doing observation work in a child development clinic. It always bothered me a little, because we sat behind windows which could be seen through only one way. Thus these children were rather defenseless because they didn't know there were any grown-ups about. They weren't under pressure to behave in ways that would preserve the illusions of their parents or other adults, and so they behaved naturally.

I saw two little boys, one of whom was in trouble. He would be about four, I suppose, and an older boy, perhaps six or a little more, was persecuting him, making him very unhappy. The smaller boy, tears in his eyes, but not quite crying, was saying, "It does so! It does so!" The bigger boy, being very superior, was saying, "It does not! Don't be silly.

It does not!" This exchange continued for a few minutes and then the little boy put his hands over his ears and said, "I won't listen to you! It does so!"

The bigger boy pulled the smaller one's hands away from his ears and hooted, "The sun does not go to bed at night. How could it go to bed? There's no bed in the sky, is there, dopey?"

The smaller child broke down, and with tears running down his face, he sobbed: "It does so go to bed at night! My daddy told me."

And at that moment he realized his father had lied to him; it was a deep tragedy, one from which he probably will never completely recover.

I don't suppose that his father even considered the question of whether he was lying to his son or not, but he was. He was misinforming the child as to the facts of life, and a child of four is very busy building a picture of his universe, building a picture of the reality in which he is going to have to learn to live. If his father, at that stage, tells him that the sun goes to bed at night, imagine how it distorts his picture of the world about him.

Now I suppose that a fabrication about the sun going to bed at night seems like a simple and harmless lie. But to the intelligent child it leads inevitably to the question "Who tucks him in?" because, when you go to bed at that age, somebody boosts you up and tucks you in, kisses you and opens the window, turns out the light. This is going to bed, and there is no other way of going to bed from a child's point of view. He is only seeking honest information when he asks this question.

What is he to be told? That the moon tucks in the sun before she comes up? Is this to become the basis of the reality that is being formed for this child at four years of age? Does any of us suppose that that child has a very good chance of ever being able to function as a world citizen with that amount of distortion at four years old? Cracks in his foundation, things out of place, things that he can't depend on? But the most important thing is that he can't depend on his father, and if he can't depend on his father to tell the truth, how can he depend on anybody?

Mistrust is the lesson that very many children learn from the habitual lies of their parents, about quite casual things that don't seem important to parents, but that are the very stones and bricks on which a child's life and relationship to reality are being built. There is no good whatever in our telling our children that they should grow up to be able to "live harmoniously in a changing total environment" if, in their small childhood, we distort the reality of the environment, if we make it nonsense to them, if we make it a place where cause and effect mean nothing, a place where thinking only gets them into the unfortunate position of not being able to trust anybody, or even their own power of observation and thinking.

This has been done to most of us when we were children, with the best of intentions, our parents not knowing any better. It was done to our parents, and to their parents, and most of the people in the world are still doing the same sort of thing to their children.

Please do not suppose that when I say that we should always tell the truth to children, I mean to suggest that the fairy tale should be rooted out. The fairy tale, the myth, the Santa Claus, all these things are charming and even valuable—as myths. What I do mean is that every child should be told, before he has a fairy story read or narrated to him, that it isn't true, so that he knows it isn't true. If he doesn't know that, the parent is not helping him to get in touch with reality.

When a child is very small, fantasy and reality are not distinct. One of the major problems that a child has to solve during his development is how to sort out fantasy and reality, so that he knows when he is dealing in real things and when he is dealing with fantasy. This is an extremely important achievement—the ability to know with certainty what is fantasy and what is reality. It forms the basis for a sound imagination—a most desirable quality, but if the lines are not clearly drawn, if the parents do not help the child to distinguish between fantasy and reality, the child may, as many people do, go on through his life without ever clearly grasping what the difference is. He will grow up without thinking in terms of cause and effect: "Who knows? A fairy may come along and fix everything up so that I need not suffer the uncomfortable results of what I did." It is easy to see that such thinking is conducive to irresponsible behavior later on.

But let us not do away with fairies and Santa Claus. Let us play them as games. Children are capable of imagining harmlessly as long as they know they are imagining. They can imagine little playmates of all kinds; they can imagine all sorts of animals, all kinds of people without any damage whatever as long as that fantasy isn't supported seriously by grownups.

We know more now than we used to about the kinds of things that handicap children's development, and we know what the needs of children are. If a small child is given sufficient food and sufficient shelter, sufficient water or moisture to stay alive, the next requirement is love; close, warm, physical-contact love.

The time has gone when psychologists and psychiatrists blushed when they used the word "love." Love has now become a scientific term (which makes it respectable) and is now recognized as a good thing. Indeed, it is now considered indispensable, or nearly so, in early childhood for effective emotional development toward maturity.

In this area, in our wonderfully advanced North America, we, oddly enough, are behind certain other cultures when it comes to loving our babies. We have acquired some rather dreadful habits—all in the name of Hygiene.

I am reminded of the time, some years ago, when I was in Pakistan, and was being guided through a very large general hospital. As we were going along a corridor, which was a sort of balcony on the side of the building, we passed the screened door to a ward. Suddenly someone pointed out to me, with great enthusiasm, something away off on the horizon in the opposite direction. Now, to any old Army inspecting officer, the situation was perfectly clear; there was something nearby they didn't want me to see. Therefore I was quite sure that whatever was hidden behind this screened door I should see. If you see only what people want you to see you will never find out anything.

So I insisted, at some risk of offense, on seeing this ward, and when I insisted, my guides began apologizing, saying that I wouldn't really like to see it at all. It was of a very old pattern; they were ashamed of it; they hoped to get it changed; they hoped that the World Health Organization might help them get the money to adopt modern and new patterns for this particular ward, because it was very bad indeed. It was a pattern hundreds of years old.

However, I still insisted that even as an antiquity I would like to see it. I went in to see this ward, with the reluctant accompaniment of the train of people with me, and I saw the best maternity ward I have ever seen in any country, far better than any I have ever seen in North America. Here was a big maternity ward with beds down both sides. The foot posts of each bed were extended up about three feet or so, and slung between the foot posts was a cradle. The baby was in the cradle, and I noticed as I looked down the ward that one squeak out of the baby and up would come the mother's foot, and with her toe she would rock the cradle. On the second squeak, which showed that the baby was really awake, she would reach into the cradle and take the baby into her arms, where a baby is supposed to be most of the time.

They wanted to get rid of that perfectly beautiful arrangement, to put their babies under glass the way we do, and to keep them in inspection wards where they can be seen at a distance by their loving fathers whenever they visit, and taken to their mother if she is good and does as the nurse tells her! They wanted to do all that because we

Westerners had given them the impression that all our methods are superior to theirs.

Those babies, if they develop an infection, recover from it twice as fast as ours do. These people are not producing little neurotic babies of one month old the way we are. Their babies do not feel themselves out in the cold world, do not feel that nobody loves them from the moment they are born, as many of ours do. Mothers in that part of the world regard as perfectly savage some of the customs they have heard about in North America where mothers actually take their babies to hospitals, leave them there, and go home. No mother in Southeast Asia would do such a thing. She would fight everybody in the hospital before she would leave her baby there and go home without it. And she is right, demonstrably right.

Whenever a baby comes to a hospital in that part of the world, the mother accompanies it, and does everything for the baby that the baby needs that doesn't require the services of a trained nurse or of a physician. The baby feels at home all the time and recovers from operation or disease much faster than ours do, and does not suffer from any neurotic disabilities as the result of illness, as ours do.

I am not suggesting that we copy all of the patterns of these other countries. We need to be discriminating about other people's customs as well as our own, but we can learn a great deal about human relations, about the upbringing of children, from these other people. Whenever we become humble enough to learn with discrimination from others' experiments in living, we will begin to progress more steadily than we are now. Unfortunately we tend to regard our own living patterns as fixed and final and of universal value and so we naturally think everyone should copy us. This is just not true.

I have been discussing the small child's need for love as a primary condition of his effective development. Any threat to love, any risk of loss of love, is for a child a nightmare, a threatening barrier between him and his continuing exploration of life. Yet, very many children run into the threat of loss of love very early in life, sometimes even within the first year. Whenever a child behaves in ways that are not acceptable to the ideas, attitudes, and moral codes of his parents (particularly of his mother), he risks running into active disapproval. This is interpreted by the child as a threat of loss of love.

The very young child is not concerned at all with the local behavior customs of the natives; he is born not knowing anything about them. One can call him uncivilized, born in sin, or just not grown up; they are all the same thing. He is a "natural," born the way he is born. And, furthermore, there are no laws anywhere saying what a child one year old should be like; he is not in any danger whatever of coming into conflict with the laws of the land and being punished for it. All he is in danger of is running into the certainties or rigidities of his parents, but there is plenty of danger in that for most children.

Most parents have rather unbending ideas about what a small child should be like, how he should behave, what he should and should not do, even about when he should do it and when he should not. Most parents will not admit that these are really only matters of convenience for themselves or for the local customs of the natives, and that they have no real universal validity whatever. When a child first begins to explore his environment—the world as he sees and feels it—he doesn't know any rules. He has no taboos. He reaches out in all directions to find out what it's like. He tries to ingest everything because this is the primitive method of getting acquainted, but he finds some things can be ingested to his advantage and some things cannot. He learns to accept and to reject, and his developing morality is based simply on what is pleasant and what is found to be unpleasant.

But even today, when very small children behave in various natural ways, parents disapprove violently. The form of behavior that gets almost certain disapproval lies in the sexual area. That is, a child, one or two years old, exploring his total environment, finds, amongst everything else in his reality, his own genital area, and it still happens (though I hope and believe not as frequently as it used to) that his mother has extremely rigid ideas about genital areas, and when the child is caught engaging in such exploration, the mother expresses disapproval very emphatically.

The child should be exploring his total environment at that stage, and there should be no taboos placed upon such exploration. This is generally acceptable, but apparently many mothers haven't been told about it, or, if they have, they can't quite believe it because of the way they have been brought up themselves. Very many children meet violence for the first time in their lives from their mother at this stage of their development. It is still common for mothers to slap a child's hand and to say to him, "Dirty! Dirty! If you do that, Mother won't love you any more."

This is a very damaging experience. The part of the child's physical equipment which is associated with basic intersexual relationship has been made dirty and its existence associated with loss of love rather than with the expression of love. This is very disturbing to the whole development of the child's relationship to the opposite sex.

As he grows older, the child is afraid to find out about sexual facts of life, because this would associate his mother and his father with the badness and dirtiness that have been imposed on him as belonging to sexual equipment. To the young child, of course, genital organs are not sexual at all, only excretory; but large areas of human behavior will have been spoiled by this early disapproval, by these attitudes imposed on a small child before his intelligence, his experience, and his freedom to think independently are sufficient for him to be able to defend himself against that type of misdirection.

This is just one example of how the intelligent child, then, at a very early age, is convinced of his sin. He is loaded with a burden of guilt, fear, and anxiety. Because the very small child, busily trying to find out everything about the total environment in which he is going to have to live, eager to explore, to know, to experiment, and enjoying very much all his urges, all the things he wants to do —the use of eyes, nose, ears, hands, fingers, feet, and legs —because this child does not naturally subscribe to Mother's rules (that is in terms of the time at which he should do things, the place where he should do them, or how he should do them—or if he should do them at all), because he runs into the threat "If you do this or don't do that, Mother won't love you any more," because he feels that what he is doing is perfectly natural to him, he reaches the conclusion that he is just naturally bad. And bad, of course, means unlovable. Mother said so. And because he dare not risk the loss of love, he learns very early in life that he must go about pretending that he isn't bad, but pretending that he is good, so that he will continue to be loved.

This is a very difficult position for a child to be in, because he can never act freely any more. He must watch all the time to see what he should do, what he is supposed to do. He knows what he naturally would do, but this has been called bad. He can hope only to learn from good people what they expect of him.

His mother, by definition, is "good" in the child's eyes, because she is what good is. She decides what is good and what is bad and is the primary authority on goodness and badness. Even God is only brought in to support the mother. He doesn't originate anything; the mother originates it. Two different mothers on opposite sides of the street may have quite different ideas of good and bad but God is made to support both of them, one just as firmly as the other.

The old saying that "Mother knows best" was regarded, and still is, in many places, as practically sacred. Few children have the temerity to ask how she knows, who told her, where she studied, what is her authority, whenever she says, "Mother knows best." Most children do not have that degree of freedom with their parents. They would be beaten down if they tried—not necessarily physically, but in one way or another. But Mother continues to make the rules.

Very many children, when these things happen to them, become very shy, afraid to face new circumstances, afraid to meet new people, afraid of the dark, afraid of all kinds of things; irrationally afraid, because they don't know how to cope with new circumstances at all. They have no confidence in natural behavior, because they have learned that natural behavior is bad and disapproved of by good people. In unknown circumstances or new situations the child is afraid to act at all for fear he will be "found out" as bad and be discarded, unloved, and unaccepted.

Thus the groundwork is laid, to a certain extent, for the beginning of the well-known inferiority complex, which those of us who have become civilized forcibly in childhood must inevitably suffer from to one degree or another. The degree will depend on the amount of fear used to train us and on how early we were beaten into conformity with the local customs of the natives, as understood by our parents.

Of course no parents deliberately do these things to their children. They do not coolly decide to hurt their children. They do not set out to impose an inferiority complex on a defenseless child. They are merely following the way they themselves were brought up, and they believe that this is the good way because it was imposed on them in childhood.

But it cannot be overemphasized that basic security comes from being loved—or more importantly—from feeling loved when one is very small. There is nothing new in this concept. Indeed, implied in all the world's great religions there has been the suggestion or the command that people should love each other, should "Love thy neighbor as thyself." The catch, of course, comes in the last bit, "as thyself." Most of us who were brought up to be moral children, good children, a credit to our parents (according to the local customs of the natives) before we were four or five or six years old, are incapable of loving ourselves, because we were convinced in early childhood that we were not naturally lovable. We could only appear to be lovable by pretending to be something other than we were. And if we cannot love ourselves in a healthy way, then it is not possible for us to really love anyone else, because we project our own hatred of ourselves on other people.

We have been talking about what not to do to children —how not to bind them to the "certainties" of the past, how not to deceive them with so-called harmless lies, how not to stunt their emotional development with the cruelest threat of all—that of the loss of love. But our responsibilities lie much deeper than a negative or even a passive level. There are certain positive things that we can and must do for our children; there are certain positive things that we can and must teach them.

Our children need to learn, early in life, values that go away beyond the advantage of the group, the father, the mother, the family, and the local natives. They can be introduced and should be introduced to world values long before they go to school, and children are capable of recognizing the existence and importance of such values if their parents show that knowledge and that feeling themselves.

We do know what teachers need in children who come to school for the first time, that is, well-educated and intelligent teachers, who are free to think for themselves. They want children who have some points of view, some knowledges, freedoms to think, children who are not nailed to the mast of an absolute belief, but who are capable of considering all peoples' attitudes and of finding what is useful in them and discarding what is not, on the initiative of their own intelligence and not because some of their ancestors said or wrote this or that, even if it was written down in a Constitution. Children need a sense of identity with the whole human race.

These are the kinds of children that are needed when they come to school. The responsibility is overwhelmingly that of the parents, who should be able to introduce their children to certain facts, to orient them reasonably effectively in relation to time, so that they do not think and feel only in the present but feel themselves part of the long processes of development, not just local time, not just since the birth of "myself" or "my father" or "my grandfather," but national time, human racial time, geological time, astronomical time. These concepts are well within the scope of a small child before he goes to school; not in detail, not in measurements or anything like that, but in knowledge that these things exist and are a part of human experience, and are the context in which man is or is not going to survive. Particularly schools need children who are already reaching forward into time, ahead of themselves.

If parents spend all their money on payments for things they can't afford, so that they never have any money, and are always being pressed or pushed and just living for the moment, their children are not going to get proper appreciation of future time. A child by the time he goes to school should, if his parents present an example, be able to save up whatever he needs for at least a week or a month ahead to get something more valuable than he could get with what he has now. Nowadays and in our present culture, by the time a boy or girl is in his early twenties or even his middle teens, he needs to be able to function about ten years ahead so that he will be able to project ahead of himself a picture of the kind of person he proposes to be after ten years or so of education and training. Otherwise he will not plan his life; he will continue to be the creature of accident in this field as well as in many other fields.

In other areas as well, such as his relation to place, a child should have learned by the time he goes to school to feel at home anywhere in space. Of course I do not mean this literally, but he should know of the existence of space and be aware of his relationship to it.

This task is much easier since the comic strips and television have "gone for" the space concept. To be sure it is somewhat distorted, but it's much better than not having any idea at all. It is very much better than the concept that many children used to get from their parents that there wasn't any place that mattered outside of the local community. It is rare to find a benefit from the comics, but this, I think, is one—that children are escaping from their locality. It may be into fantasy, but still it is an enlargement of experience beyond local boundaries.

In relation to things, children have a great deal of developing to do. When they are born, their relation to things is entirely ingestive. It is just that they want to absorb anything that can be absorbed, as an amoeba does, in the most primitive way of coping with things. A lot of people continue to be amoebas all their lives, trying to get hold of and incorporate anything they can; just to have stuff and things is regarded as of itself creditable and productive of a feeling of superiority. A child should be able to be relatively independent of things by the time he goes to school. At least, he should be able to discriminate between things which are just temporarily amusing and those which are really permanently valuable. Again this is a responsibility of his parents.

A child's relationship with persons is of such generally recognized importance that it needs no lengthy discussion here. We are all aware that a child's relationship to persons all through his life will be very largely determined during the first weeks and months of his life by his relationship with his mother or the substitute for his mother.

The greatest service that parents can give their children is to help them to reach reality, reality as it is known at the present time, and to give them the freedom to change this reality, to change their attitudes as more knowledge becomes available, to adjust to changed circumstances without guilt, without feelings of sin, without anxiety, and without being afraid to think naturally or to accept their own naturalness. If we can give our children this, then undoubtedly they will be able to develop away beyond our level of maturity, become much more mature than we have been or can hope to be because of the handicaps of our particular upbringing.

THE UNITED NATIONS:
A MEANS, NOT AN END

Wᴇ ʜᴀᴠᴇ ᴛᴏᴜᴄʜᴇᴅ on some of the problems now facing the world, some of the reactions that human beings tend to have when faced with situations they feel they can't handle adequately, the regressive tendencies that we see in many parts of the world today. There are many types of regression. We see people going back toward more primitive types of behavior in all fields—social, economic, religious, and political.

At the same time, we also see some constructive reactions to the pervasive anxiety that is being felt by very large numbers of people throughout the world. We see some people moving forward, really trying to face the realities of the world as it is now, trying to develop themselves and their culture to the point where they will be able to cope with these difficulties more effectively.

Among these constructive efforts, and, perhaps the most important, is the setting up of the United Nations and its family of agencies. The United Nations is the latest step, after a long series of experiments, in human cooperation.

People have been trying to learn how to live together for a very long time—first only in small groups, but gradually in larger and larger groups. Eventually, through the League of Nations, the first attempt was made to live on a world scale and on a world stage.

That experiment was weak. It was not sufficiently well set up. It was not widely or strongly enough supported, and therefore could not do its job effectively.

However, even if the League of Nations' only contribution had been its experimental work in international organization, the result justified its existence, for the bitter experience taught us how to set up the United Nations. Actually, the League of Nations did much more than that. Consider its work in international health, which it did extremely well. It was limited in its scope, but some very fine work was done that has lasted until now, and has formed a basis for continuing work in international health.

Near the end of the Second World War, it became evident that something stronger than the League of Nations would have to be set up. It became quite clear that no nation would ever again be able to defend itself or ensure security for its people by itself. It was quite clear that something had to be done that had not been done before, or, at least, done to an extent not known before, if we were to be able to hope for any satisfactory degree of security in the future.

We began to get concerned not just about other people and how they might behave, but also about ourselves and how we might behave. We began to question ourselves, and many of us came to realize that we were dangerous people, that we could ourselves be dangerous to human survival, that the behavior patterns of our ancestors, carried on only one more generation, or perhaps less, might destroy us all.

It was under the influence of this pervasive anxiety that the nations of the world came together and set up the United Nations. This was a good thing; it offered hope for the human race. But after the United Nations was set up, too many of us decided that we had done our duty by the human race, and that we could just go home and enjoy ourselves as we always had before. The United Nations would see that nobody fought anybody else, would see that nobody was hungry, would see that nobody encroached on anybody else's territory, and would introduce the happy world that everybody hoped could be made. This, of course, is absurd.

Such a hope became even more absurd when many of us showed that we expected this all to be done cheaply, that we thought it wouldn't cost us anything to speak of. Oh yes, we were prepared to have our governments contribute a few million dollars, or even more, provided this wouldn't affect our own standard of living to any degree or hurt our individual pocketbooks. Most of us expected to buy security for the human race at almost no cost—an obvious impossibility.

We are only now beginning to realize that the cost of security is going to be very great, not just in terms of money, but in terms that are dearer to us than money: loyalties, certainties that have been part of our upbringing, absolutes that were imposed early in life, the certainties of our ancestors that may no longer be appropriate. It is beginning to dawn on many people in many parts of the world that it is in this kind of coinage that security will be bought, if we are to find security at all. It cannot be done just by providing dollars or materials or food, though they too are necessary in enormous quantities.

The United Nations and its specialized agencies were admirably designed for a specific purpose—a very specific and limited purpose. They were very carefully kept from becoming supranational organizations. They were designed to be instruments, and instruments only, to take their instructions from the governments of the world, and to do exactly as they were told to do by the peoples of the world through their governments. The United Nations is not capable of doing anything other than what it is told to do by its rulers, who are the governments of the world.

It is perfectly competent to do that job—what it is told to do. However, there are people who believe that everything could be fixed and all problems nicely handled simply by changing or amending or enlarging in some way the Charter of the United Nations.

This, I should think, is very questionable. The United Nations and its agencies have constitutions that are at least a generation ahead of the world's present inhabitants. If nations want to do something constructive, then constitutions will not stop them.

Although the Charter of the United Nations and the constitutions of the specialized agencies are quite adequate for quite a long time yet, many nations have tried, and do try, to use the United Nations, and sometimes even one or another of the specialized agencies, for purposes other than those for which they were designed—for competitive purposes, in order to gain prestige or power or economic advantage for themselves, or political domination over someone else, or in some way to get more security for themselves at the expense of the security of some other groups. These purposes are all foreign to the intentions and design of the United Nations, which is simply and purely to help the nations achieve mutual cooperation. Thus, whenever any government or group of governments tries to use the United Nations or its specialized agencies for any lesser purpose, for the advantage of any nation or any group of nations, the mechanism doesn't work very well, because it wasn't designed to work well for those purposes.

Very frequently, one hears the United Nations criticized as a debating society. Of course the United Nations is a debating society. That's primarily what it is for. It is there to provide an opportunity for governments to talk out the world's problems. It is a place where your representatives and mine go to tell the people of the world, and show them, what we are like at home, to reflect a picture of the peoples of our countries. Our difficulties, our generosities, our selfishnesses, our nationalistic attitudes, or prejudices of all kinds, our taboos—all these things are brought out and illustrated to other peoples of the world. Far from deserving criticism, this is an extremely valuable function. For in the United Nations our representatives can learn firsthand what the people are like with whom we have to live effectively, peacefully, and harmoniously during our generation.

Many people might accept the idea of the debating

society but interpret it to mean that the United Nations is a place where we go to reproach other people for being the way they are. This is an old, old habit. Man's method of dealing with difficulties in the past has always been to tell everyone else how they should behave. We've all been doing that for centuries.

It should be clear by now that this no longer does any good. Everybody has by now been told by everybody else how he should behave; therefore, everybody knows how everybody else thinks he should behave. The criticism is not effective; it never has been, and it never is going to be. There is only one telling that is effective—our telling ourselves how to behave.

Of course it is much more comfortable to tell other people. It's much more pleasant, because whenever you tell other people how they should behave, you feel superior. It's very pleasant to feel superior and feel that you know more about a lot of things than other people do. That's one reason why people write books—so they can tell other people how they should behave.

It is because we so love telling others what to do that we have difficulty in getting along with so-called underdeveloped people to their—or our—advantage. For example, many of our best-intentioned, nicest people have gone into other people's countries and felt that the first thing they had to do was to get clothes on these other people. Why? Just because we have puritanical ideas about uncovered bodies. We make these other people feel ashamed by telling them it is "wrong" to go about the way they do, without enough clothes on.

We are not doing those people a service in acting so. True, we may sell them a lot of cotton or wool and add to our profits and help ourselves economically, but actually we are sacrificing those people to our economic conditions, although we don't realize it. People that insist on poor unfortunate natives in a hot climate wearing clothes all over their bodies all of the time don't know what they are doing or why they are doing it.

There is an old saying that we damn the sin we have no mind to, which, like many old saying, is totally untrue. We damn the sins that we do have a mind to, only we don't want to admit that we do or can't let ourselves recognize our own desires. It is those "sins," those kinds of behavior, that we have had to repress early in our own experience, that we are so forcibly determined to fight in other people when we see them. We are irritated when other people are allowed to behave in ways that we secretly would like to, but cannot because they are forbidden to us.

I think there is no doubt that this idea of sin creates much havoc in our relationships with other cultures, and that we should begin to think far more clearly and more extensively than we have in the past about it. We must remember that it is only in some cultures that sin exists. For instance, the Eskimos didn't have this concept until quite recently. Now they have; they caught it from us.

A friend of mine came down from the East Arctic once with a very eminent cleric, who was talking about the troubles he had had with the Eskimos. He said, "You know, for years we couldn't do anything with those Eskimos at all; they didn't have any sin. We had to teach them sin for years before we could do anything with them." The Eskimos were in a state of innocence, but they had to be made to feel sinful so they could be controlled.

This bears thinking about. What is this concept of sin for? To me it is very clear, if we really look at it. Calling people bad, labeling them bad, convincing them that they are bad, is just an expression of our attempt to control them, to make them behave in the ways we want them to behave.

If we had lived in another time or place, if we had been born a hundred years earlier or a hundred years later, or on the other side of a river, or a mountain or an ocean, the badnesses and goodnesses would have been quite differently distributed. We would subscribe just as heartily to quite a different set of certainties of which we would be just as sure and to which we would be equally devoted.

This is the way in which the human race has developed throughout history. Each person has had imposed on him in childhood the absolute certainties of local customs of the natives, whatever those might chance to be. If we look at ourselves—and I'm not suggesting that we look at anybody else, but just at ourselves—we find that what we have really done is to accept a whole set of certainties, and local prejudices and possibly, after a long lifetime of what we call hard thinking, have made only some minor rearrangement of those prejudices. This is about the most that we usually expect from ourselves.

But it is clear today that this just isn't good enough any longer. We are going to have to decide that, although some of the things we have been teaching our children should be preserved, there are some that should be discarded. We can no longer assume that it is our given duty to tell everyone else in the world how they should behave, as we all have been doing for centuries. It is rather for us to convince other people by our own example, to show them by our own behavior that our kind of thinking and our attitudes are worth considering and emulating, but not just by telling them or by trying to knock down their beliefs.

It is easy for us to be all-seeing and all-knowing about other people's beliefs. It is easy for us to say, as people do, that India should get rid of the sacred cows, because these cows destroy enough food to feed about twenty million people. We have been told that in India, if there is a shortage of food, a child will die of starvation but not a cow, because the child isn't sacred and the cow is. But there is no good whatever in telling the Hindu to get rid of the cow, because it is sacred, and nobody gets rid of anything sacred because somebody else tells him to. Nobody, including ourselves, ever has; nobody, including ourselves, ever will; not if it is regarded as sacred. One does not deal with such things by instruction. There is no way of beating people—even if only verbally—into behaving in particular ways.

There are those of us who might agree to leave the great masses of other people from other cultures alone but who think that we have the right to instruct their leaders. We should instruct their leaders that, instead of shaking their fists at us, they should shake their fists at their own kind. We should tell their leaders to limit their great populations that we so nobly are trying to help feed, to instruct their leaders to come to grips with the fact in their own countries. This idea is equally futile. Leaders don't take instruction very well from foreigners.

I do not mean here to condemn all who want to go to a foreign, "underdeveloped" land and work among and help its people. There are many who are sincerely devoted to the cause of improving the human condition. But there are certain personal qualifications necessary for the individual who wishes to cross into other cultures and work in other areas.

If you wish to work in the field of public health, it goes without saying that an adequate technical knowledge is essential. But given this adequate degree of technical knowledge, personality is immeasurably more important than a very high degree of technical knowledge. Most of the failures of communication, most of the failures to help people adapt and adopt our techniques are the result of personal failures—failures in personality and not failures of technique.

When anyone presumes to go into another country and mess about with other people's lives, he is assuming considerable responsibility. He needs to be quite sure that what he is doing is really for the good of those people and is not just something which he believes should be emulated by those people because we ourselves live that way. The first necessity in going into another country is to recognize exactly where those people are in their development, what they are like, and then to visualize the next appropriate step in the direction in which those people want to go, because they, too, are entitled to their experiments, just as much as we are, and their best course or next step is not necessarily at all the way in which we have gone.

For instance, in the medical field, there has been a tendency on the part of people from Europe and America to go to the underdeveloped countries and teach the people there to get on with their medical development in the same way we have. This may be quite absurd, because we have medical care developed to a level that is not going to be possible for those people for generations. We are superimposing our highly developed methods of treatment on them without first showing them the long, slow methods of prevention, forgetting that we did nothing but treat diseases for hundreds of years with almost no techniques of prevention at all.

Thus, the way the so-called underdeveloped countries should develop is by prevention first, with treatment when they can sustain it, or to the degree that they can sustain it. Prevention is wholesale; treatment is retail. We may have to sell our wares by undertaking treatment, by using penicillin, for instance, for the apparently magical cure of yaws or other diseases, but the primary necessity is prevention.

It is often difficult for people from highly developed countries to recognize that the needs of people to whom they go are not necessarily the needs of their own cultures. Again a freedom of attitude, an ability to recognize different circumstances, an ability to respect the sacrednesses of other people is important.

The kind of person who works best among peoples of other cultures is the person who is earnest, devoted, and unselfish, who goes to these people, lives with them, never hurting their feelings, never trying to instruct them; he first makes himself liked and trusted because he never criticizes but rather helps them to assume responsibility for doing the things that need to be done in their country. The kind of person who works best in cultures foreign to his own is the person who learns most while he is in those cultures, who enjoys working in them tremendously, not because the work is easy—often it is very difficult and even exhausting—but because he has himself grown extensively. No person who is frozen in his attitudes can expect to be helpful in another culture. No person who goes to another culture to impose his own certainties on it can really be helpful. The person who can help them to take the next necessary appropriate steps in the direction of their own intentions is the kind of person who is valuable. Nobody accepts anything because it is good for him. People accept things if they like the person who brings them. It's as simple as that.

I believe that the methods that the United Nations and its specialized agencies are now employing are effective methods of helping those people. To be sure, there are difficulties in the setup of the United Nations, because when the United Nations was established, it represented little more than a hope—a hope that the nations of the world might be able to live up to the intentions expressed in its Charter and the constitutions of its specialized agencies. That hope has been only to some extent justified—not nearly enough to guarantee any reasonable degree of security.

The United Nations Charter and the constitutions of all the specialized agencies may be seen as a minimum prescription, for this generation, for a sufficient degree of security to justify the hope that the peoples of the world may continue to exist and get on with their job of evolution. They do not represent any final prescription by any means, because, by the next generation, human development will need to extend far beyond the limits prescribed in the present constitutions. But for this generation, we may regard these statements by the peoples of the world as the minimum necessity. Most of us have not yet begun to recognize the implications of that fact in relation to our own lives.

The constitutions state, sometimes in very clear terms, the necessary changes in the attitudes and lives that must take place if the human race is to go on developing. None of these statements, I suppose, is new, but the thing that is new is that they have been agreed to by practically all the nations of the world.

The statement in the Constitution of UNESCO, for instance, about wars—UNESCO is the United Nations Economic and Social Council, and in its Constitution is a very simple statement that says that wars begin in the minds of men.

Of course, everybody has always known this, but it's something that we have been refusing to look at. We have been blaming wars on economic pressures. We have been blaming them on all kinds of things outside man's habitual patterns of thinking, and it is in man's thinking that we are going to have to look for the causes of war. True, there are complications of food supply and all sorts of economic pressures, and so on, but the fact is that warfare does not provide any solution for any of those problems, and it hasn't provided any solution for several generations.

It could at one time. Warfare was extremely useful to some people. Of course, it made life a little difficult, if possible at all, for others, but in the days when one tribe was short of cattle and women, and they could raid another tribe and replenish their supplies, war was a very useful way of behaving. It was accepted as perfectly normal human behavior, and even advantageous—at least to the people who won the war. In the past, it was possible to win a war, as it isn't now, and never will be again.

Because war was advantageous and desirable to many people, acceptance of warfare as normal has been one of the attitudes that most of us have accepted early in our lives. We have taken for granted that war comes and goes; these things just happen. We have also tended to take for granted that there was nothing much that we could do about it, and, to a certain extent, this was true.

It would seem that it is the incorporation in man's mind of the belief that war is normal that has had so much to do with this succession of wars that has been going on. It has been regarded as not respectable to suggest that one's own country should not go to war if its dignity is affronted or if its prestige is hurt or its honor questioned, or if somebody tries to grab some of its territory. It is only recently that we have been able to question the desirability of war without being called a traitor or subversive, or whatever word happens to be in fashion at the time for keeping people from saying what they think.

In the World Health Organization's Constitution, the one that I know best, there are also statements that indicate some new points of view. One is a definition of the word "health." This is the opening statement in the Constitution of the World Health Organization. It has certain importance, because this statement has been agreed to under a signed and ratified international convention on behalf of practically all the people in the world, by some eighty-eight nations.

This definition of health is very authoritative. It would require a two-thirds vote of the nations of the world to change the meaning of the word, so it is a word about which the makers of dictionaries won't have any trouble at all.

In the Constitution of the World Health Organization, health is defined, by the nations of the world, as: "A state of complete physical, mental, and social well being, and not merely the absence of disease or infirmity."

This is a big order. It suggests the responsibility of our generation to develop a degree of maturity that has never been expected before of any human generation. Never were our ancestors confronted by any such requirement in their development, but this definition suggests that from now on we are going to have to develop well beyond the level that was expected of any of our ancestors, that we have further to go in our march toward maturity than was ever required before.

In case there's any doubt of that, there's another definition just a little later in that same Constitution, about children. Personally, I'm not very happy about this definition, because it was made by rather elderly people, and in it we suggest rather frightening responsibilities for the next generation, but none for us. The attitude it suggests is that nobody should expect us old people, who have white hair— or very little hair, if any—to change our minds or start to think in new ways or learn new tricks in interhuman relations, because it's perfectly well known that, as we age, our minds get stiff, and it's very difficult to force them into new channels. This is a very nice "out" for those of us who don't want to undertake this extremely difficult process, new to most of us, of thinking.

The statement I refer to is the one about the development of children, and, as I said before, it's rather frightening. It says:

"Healthy development" ("healthy," of course, meaning physically, mentally, and socially) "of the child is of basic importance"; and then it goes on: "the ability to live harmoniously in a changing total environment is essential to such development."

How is that for a goal of development for the next generation?

But you will notice that it only applies to children. They are expected by the old people of the world to learn to live harmoniously in a changing total environment with everybody in the world, whereas their parents, in many cases, are not able even to live harmoniously in their own families, with people whom they have known all their lives. This is even a bigger order, but again, I think, we must accept the fact that these things are written as minimum prescriptions for our security and survival.

It is obvious that to implement what these constitutions say is an enormous job. It is not going to be done effectively or completely in one generation, but we do need to recognize at least the weight of our responsibility in this generation. We need to recognize the fact that we are the first generation of the human race to hold a veto power over the continuing existence of the human race. This has never been true of any of our ancestors before, but it is true for us.

It is in the light of this reality that we must begin to look at the world's problems. And if we really look at them honestly—or as honestly as we can—many of us, perhaps with some regret or even astonishment, will come to the conclusion that we and people like us are contributing to their existence.

This would be very easy to demonstrate if we could only go around to the other side of the world and look at ourselves from there. Of course, nobody can see his own culture clearly from the inside, because every culture provides distorting glasses through which all the members of that culture see themselves and the world. That is a part of what cultures are: a set of attitudes, a set of points of view which are native to and current in a particular group of people.

We only have to use our imaginations to get out of our culture and look at it from some other place, to recognize that it might possibly be that even we, the nice people of North America, are a problem to other people.

Earlier I have touched briefly on some of the areas

wherein we may appear to be a problem: our wastefulness, the extravagance with which we expend the earth's irreplaceable natural resources; and the fact that we are not doing very much to even the balance, nothing that is really very constructive yet, because we believe that our first obligation is to ourselves, and that what we must do first is to maintain and raise our own high standard of living.

No wonder we are regarded as a problem. No wonder we are not regarded with any great degree of admiration from other places.

Of course they admire some things about us. But mostly what they admire, I'm afraid, are our ancestors. We had the most admirable, nicest, most aggressive ancestors that anybody ever had. They went out while the going was good, and grabbed off the best parts of the world before the rules were changed. This is regarded as highly admirable in many parts of the world where people regret that their ancestors didn't grab while the going was good, before the rules were changed, but instead sat back and left future generations to suffer the results of their lack of action.

Perhaps our smug and comfortable beliefs in our own admirability may not be so well justified as most of us have heretofore taken for granted. Perhaps our conviction that we are so admirable that all anyone needs to do in order to be right is to imitate us is irrational in the eyes of other people. It would seem well to remember that behind every threat to security in the world today is to be found irrational thinking, thinking based on early learned certainties, on traditional points of view, early imposed loyalties, absolutes of all kinds, taboos or social pressures that are inherent in a particular culture and which make impossible understanding other kinds of people and viewing sympathetically their problems and the world's problems.

In the United Nations, quite frequently delegates speak in more mature, more civilized, more world-minded ways, than their people at home or their governments will support. It has happened a good many times that individuals have been withdrawn from delegations—taken home—because they were doing their job too well. They were doing what they were supposed to do, what they were there to do, but their people at home didn't want it done. Their people at home generally wanted their own advantage considered first. It has also happened, a good many times, that delegates come to their friends from other countries and apologize for statements they are about to make under instructions from their own governments. When I was with the World Health Organization, not once, but many times, delegates came to me saying that they were very sorry but they had instructions to make such and such a statement, knowing as they did that it would make trouble and that it was concerned with the prestige or advantage of their own country and not with the welfare of the people of the world. They were ashamed. They were ashamed in the eyes of their friends from other parts of the world, but there was nothing they could do about it. They were unhappy and embarrassed by these instructions from their governments, from their state departments, from their foreign offices, because they knew that these statements were founded on the desire of their governments to get advantage over somebody else, which is not what they are supposed to be in the United Nations meetings to do.

I have also seen many members of secretariats come back

to work from home leaves very unhappy indeed. I remember one man telling me that he didn't know how he was ever going to be able to go home to live, because he found it very painful living among his own relatives. He said, "Those people are still worried about what kind of car they're going to get next year," which, he thought, was rather an odd concern to have in a world in the state that ours is in now. He had had the illusion that the people at home had been growing up as fast as he, and they hadn't, and when he went home he felt himself among strangers, because their attitudes and their points of view were no longer his. He had become a functioning world citizen.

To many, this is the same thing as subversion; it is labeled and thought of as disloyalty. Actually, it is an expanded loyalty, a more important loyalty, a far more valid loyalty— a loyalty to the welfare of the peoples of the world.

If the people at home react in these ways, it would appear that we can't, at this time, expect too much from the United Nations and its specialized agencies. They can go on at about the level they are on now, they can do good work, and there is a great deal of work to do. But until the people at home do some growing up and begin to understand the necessities of this generation, we can't expect United Nations and its specialized agencies to take very many steps forward in bringing about world cooperation for mutual benefit.

The nations of the world are the people of the world, and as long as the people of the world believe that the United Nations can save the world by itself, without any very great investment from themselves, there is not much hope for the United Nations going beyond where it is now. It would be much more comfortable just to let the diplomats do it, but it just won't work that way. The great job that has to be done cannot be left only to the diplomats. We have to do it ourselves. We must look at facts, face reality, and recognize that the next steps have to be taken in the homes and the schools and the churches of the world.

In many countries I have visited in recent years, people have come to me and asked how to get a job in the United Nations. They want to do something significant, something important for the welfare of the world. The answer to that I have, I think, made very clear: "Go home and do it, because it is at home that the job needs to be done. That is where the lag is, not in the United Nations. That is where the catching up has to be done."

Any absolute, any imposed loyalty that cannot be changed, any certainty given to children that cannot be thought about, only accepted, any taboo hedged about with threat and fear and anxiety—these prevent our implementing the constitutions of the United Nations and its specialized agencies, because the United Nations can do only what the peoples of the world tell it to do. It has no initiative of its own, it has no personality of its own, it has no existence of its own. It is purely the embodied intention and will of the peoples of the world, and is merely an instrument—admirably designed—to carry out the instructions of the world's nations within a framework of world cooperation rather than within a framework of chauvinistic competition.

IMAGINATION AS THE
TOOL OF REALITY

We have been trying to understand some of the disabilities, as well as some of the abilities, of mankind at this present moment in human history, when circumstances have changed beyond all knowledge familiar or available to our ancestors. In trying to understand better what our problems are and how best to face them, it is necessary for us to look frequently at our ancestors and their attitudes. This is not to be unkind or critical about our ancestors, because, for their time and place, considering the knowledge available to them and their comparatively limited experience, they did astonishingly well. But also it is true that they had attitudes that are not useful to us now, and many such attitudes we are going to have to learn to discard or to change or revise in ways that we find desirable for harmonious living in our kind of world.

One of the habits of our ancestors, dating back as far as we know anything about the human race, is recognizably responsible for many of our present and past difficulties. That is the habit that our ancestors had, ever since the

beginning, as far as we know, of filling in the blank spaces
in their experience with hobgoblins and demons and other
such creatures. Wherever there was an area that they didn't
understand, wherever there was something unknown, somebody could be counted on to invent a content for it, to
create an explanation for it. So we have found that all the
unknown areas have at one time or another been filled
with magics, with demons and devils and gods and dragons,
and many of the people of the world still inherit the concept of the unknown that was imposed on their ancestors.

Of course man was afraid of the dark; of course man was
afraid of unknown territory; there might be something in
it which might do him harm. He didn't know what might
come at him from any direction. His ideas about move-
ment, about transportation, were, of course, very incom-
plete. This propensity of our ancestors toward magics was
carried on right up to recent times and written down in
books as recently as the last two or three hundred years.
Even cartographers, relatively objective people, were in the
habit, when they were making maps, of filling in the unknown parts with pictures of dragons and fantastic fish, and
all sorts of queer-looking people, because legend told them
that this was a place of phoenixes, or man-eating trees, or
all sorts of hybrid creatures.

Unfortunately many people learned to capitalize on
these inventions. When one of our ancestors invented a
concept for an unknown area of human experience, he was
greatly admired, because he presumably knew a lot more
than anybody else did, and it was always possible to capitalize on such inventions by raising taboos around them, by

defending them with threats of revenge on the part of gods or devils, by using magics of all kinds. Such methods effectively frighten people from real exploration of that area of experience, if the taboos are imposed in childhood.

All our ancestors at one stage or another believed in spirits. They believed in unknown personalities, and projected their own traits and attitudes on these unknown spirits that inhabited trees, rocks, lakes, mountains, weather; almost anything was personalized. Then various ways were invented of coping with these invented spirits, to placate them, to please them, to plead before them, even to threaten them, or bribe them in some way or other, by means of ritual or by behavior patterns presumed to be, and taught to be, pleasing to these unknown spirits.

We have a hangover from those days still with us. We have remnants of those attitudes which still influence the attitudes of many of us throughout the world. Only recently I heard a doctor say something about his health being in fine condition, and then, quite unobtrusively, he touched wood.

This is astonishing, perfectly astonishing. This doctor is a very intelligent man and knows a lot of things. He knows a great many things I wish I knew. How can he believe that he is better off if he touches wood after he has boasted of his good health than if he doesn't? What kind of mental process goes on within him? Who is going to do what about his boasting that his health is good? How is he threatened? What presence is there who will hear him say that he is very fortunate that he hasn't had a cold all winter and who will spitefully send him a humdinger of a cold? And how and why will that presence be placated or blackmailed, or whatever it is, by his touching wood?

How many of our attitudes, how many of our points of view are determined by the magic thinking of our ancestors? I am afraid that we would have to come to the conclusion that many of our attitudes are so determined, or at least influenced. All around us we see the reality of our failure to develop anything like the knowledge that is now available to us. We are still going on being extraordinarily primitive, extraordinarily amenable to magic, to total irresponsibility from an intellectual point of view. Can anyone who touches wood be expected to function rationally in other areas of his life?

The astonishing thing is that some people can be totally irrational about some things and at the same time be reasonably rational about something else, but to do so they must divide their personality, split it. They must teach themselves not to think about certain things. They must develop blind spots in their personality. Such persons can expect adequate and effective functioning from only a part of their total personality, because undoubtedly all that part of anybody that induces him to touch wood or to avoid the number thirteen or to be upset on seeing a black cat or to avoid walking under a ladder (even if there isn't any painter on it) cannot function adequately.

These are only illustrations of the degree and the variety of irrationalities that are part of the personalities of very many of us, even now at this advanced stage of human development. That is to say, that part of us has developed, part of our intellect has developed, but other parts of ourselves have stayed at very primitive levels.

But by now we should have reached the stage where it

should be possible for us to stop trying to account for things that we are not capable of accounting for, recognizing that there are areas of man's development, where he came from and where he is going, that we cannot know with our present knowledge. It may be that in another million years or so man will have developed his abilities to learn a great deal more. It may be that some of the aspects of human experience that are blank or unknown now will be filled in by knowledges gained by our descendants, by experiences that they may have that we do not now have. It seems very important indeed that we should learn to accept and learn to live with our ignorance and not go on filling in the blanks with magics of varying sorts.

Let us realize and accept the fact that we are ignorant about a great many things. A few hundred years ago, in the Middle Ages, all things were known; everything was in the book—certainly in Christian countries—and it was regarded as heretical to question anything that was known. Any attempt to advance knowledge was regarded as an attack on the orthodoxies of the time. That has been true in many parts of the world at many times, because orthodoxies have set up beliefs appropriate to one stage of development, but then they are frozen and not allowed to develop further, not allowed to grow with the advancing stage of knowledge.

Orthodoxies or dogmas expressed in the attitudes acceptable to our remote ancestors may or may not be acceptable to us now. And we should be the judges of what we will or will not accept, because we do know more now than our ancestors ever knew before. Some such dogmas may continue to be valid, in that they are still reasonable in relation to the knowledge that we continue to gain all the time; some of them may be found to be valid from a scientific point of view. But if we find that some of the attitudes of our ancestors do not fit our world as it is today, we should surely do our ancestors the honor of believing that if they were here now they would have the sense to change their minds, and would no longer see things the same way they did many years ago.

However, most people insist on rigidifying the great prophets and teachers, forgetting that every one of them was a rebel in his own time, was thinking experimentally, was reinterpreting the concept of God, trying to bring it up to the concepts available to the people of his time and place. The trouble with old concepts is that they become fixed, yet, if their original propagators could return today, they would not express their attitudes in the same words at all, because they would also have the additional evidence, the new experiences, that we now have. The most damaging thing that has been done to religion has been the deep-freezing of the great prophets, the not allowing their concepts to change after they have died, the forgetting that in their time and place they were all rebels.

But I do not want to give the impression that I am placing upon religions alone the full blame for the fixed attitudes, the rigid certainties, the unchanging beliefs in ancient prophets that plague the world today. We also have with us the political "isms" and even those of fairly recent origin are weighted with ironclad rules and standards. Political "isms" too are faiths developed in a particular time and a particular place and couched in terms that were appropriate to one man's experience of that time and place.

Consider Karl Marx, for example. The conclusions reached by him under the circumstances he knew are not applicable to the world as it is now. There is a lot of evidence available today that was not available to Marx. He did an astonishing job of thinking from his own spot in history, but his predictions were unsound. Things didn't turn out the way that he said they would, and the conditions that he set up for progress and for development have not been justified. They have been shown to be untrue.

Therefore, I think it is not possible to believe in the substance of Marx. He tried hard, and I think he did a great job for his particular time and place, but he too, has been frozen. If Marx were alive now he would have a great deal of evidence available that he didn't have available during his lifetime. There has been much experience since then, and I do not think that Marx would subscribe to his own writings if he were alive today. I am sure we would find him changed very drastically indeed.

What we the people of the world need, perhaps most, is to exercise our imaginations, to develop our ability to look at things from outside our accidental area of being. This is a form of exercise that would do all of us good—to go to work on our imaginations and, every once in a while, to take them out for a good run. Most of us have never taken out our imaginations for any kind of run in all our lives. They have been tied up tightly to some set of original premises into which we happened to be born, premises which control our imaginations almost entirely.

Whenever we invent hobgoblins and magics to people

the dark, unknown areas of our environment (magics that we sometimes convert into orthodoxies), we are abusing what is perhaps one of the most precious faculties that we, as human beings, possess. We are giving a negative, sterile use to our wonderful imaginations.

Imagination is an extremely valuable instrument—if it is free, if it is allowed to tell the truth, if it doesn't deal in fantasy and myth and magics, but deals in realities. Imagination can be a scout that we send into unknown territory to bring back true reports of what it would be like if we went there and behaved in this way or in that way—or if we didn't behave at all.

But most people's imaginations are not able to bring back true reports, because they have been crippled or blinded, in some way or other, or mutilated in childhood; certain subjects, certain areas of human behavior, certain points of view have been tabooed, have been labeled in such a way that one's imagination isn't allowed to exercise itself in those fields. For many people those taboos cover very large areas of life.

The result, of course, is the same as it would be for a military commander to send out scouts, telling them not to report on, say, anything green or anything wet, or anything else that might be objectionable to the commanding officer. Naturally, the reports he got back would not be reliable, and that is the case when most people try to use their imaginations.

But before we fully discuss the exploratory function of imagination, let us first consider another function—the safety-valve function. Imagination, as well as being a scout which should bring back true information, also has a very important safety-valve function, the judicious use of which should make it possible for us to get along with the queer customs of the local natives with whom we all have to get along. One should be able to use a free and active imagination to obtain at least partial emotional satisfaction in ways quite unacceptable to the local customs of the natives, which, after all, are only local and temporary and which may be changed anyway after a few years. Imagination, then, should not be bound to the local certainties of any group of natives. It should be free.

It is easy to give examples. I remember a man I knew years ago who had great difficulty in using the back part of his house. He couldn't go out the back door and through a sort of shed at the rear at all. He had to come in the front door and go out the front door. It was rather embarrassing —as well as inconvenient.

He would escort his wife from the garage to the back door, and then would make excuses for going around and coming in the front door himself. He didn't know why he did this at all, and it took quite a while to discover what the trouble was. After much difficulty, he found that what he really feared was an ax hanging on the wall of the shed. He didn't know why he was so afraid of the ax; consciously he had been afraid only of the back part of the house. Eventually he found the source of his anxiety and fear; with a very great deal of effort he discovered why he was afraid of the ax. He was not afraid that it would fall on him; he was afraid he would take it upstairs and chop up his wife.

Well, his wife was the kind of person who should have

been chopped up, and this poor man wouldn't let himself realize what she was really like.

An active reliable imagination under those circumstances goes through an effective drill which can help take the tension out of such a situation. If a man has that kind of wife, then he can imagine going down, getting the ax and sharpening it on a grindstone, and taking it upstairs and murdering his wife. And it makes him feel very good while he's doing it.

But, given a good, active, effective imagination that tells the truth, he then realizes that if he were really to do this, he would have an "indisposable" body—or pieces of it—on his hands that might prove very embarrassing, and he decides that it wouldn't be a good thing to do after all. In the meantime, however, he has had his fun, and he can now use the back door. He isn't going to have any more trouble about that. All this man had to do to cure himself was to chop his wife up about once a week at first, then gradually taper off to about once a month. Of course I oversimplify this illustration.

This is an example of the kind of thing that many of us do not let ourselves do. Instead we swallow our hostility, and hostility is notably indigestible. Of course, there are other ways of coping with hostility. Some people, if they are spoken to in an unkindly way by their employer, talk back and get fired. But they find after a while that it isn't a good idea to talk back, so instead they take their hostility out on their secretary and send her home in tears, and of course she takes out her hostility on somebody else if she can. Others, who are too civilized to be hostile in public, go home and beat their wives, in one way or another, or make sudden and harsh demands on their children, and feel much better afterwards, if a little ashamed. Still others, who are too civilized to beat up their wives or abuse their children, go into the cupboard and throw their shoes around, or assault the cat or the dog or swear at the canary.

But those who consider themselves really deeply civilized do none of those things, either in reality or in imagination. They swallow their hostility and keep it inside themselves. Hostility, however, is poisonous. It's true that the effects of the poison may not show for quite a long time. At first it may be only temper tantrums, or gastric ulcers (which aren't too much trouble), or pains in the back, or headache, or palpitation of heart, or chronic constipation, or diarrhea, or nervous tensions. Sooner or later, the poison will show some effects. Imagination isn't necessarily the best way of treating hostility; it isn't completely satisfying, particularly to emotion that has been suppressed for some time; but if hostility is used up as one goes along, the imagination method of treatment is reasonably satisfactory —reasonably so, not completely. Obviously, the most satisfactory way to deal with someone you dislike is to knock him on the head with a big rock, there's no doubt about it. The most satisfying way of using up an urge is to do exactly as the urge would indicate the first moment it shows its head. But the results would be very uncomfortable. Such behavior would produce complete chaos and a state of anxiety and fear on the part of human beings which, in our present numbers, would be socially disastrous.

We have made laws which are simply arrangements between people about desirable behavior. As soon as individuals of the human race began to live in the same bit of woods together, they had to make some sort of mutual arrangements about how they should behave, in order not to be terrified all the time. And so, we make, and we continue to make, arrangements about our behavior to which we mutually subscribe generally. Each one of these arrangements is in control of some natural human urge. Otherwise it wouldn't be necessary to have any laws at all.

Therefore, we have to find substitute ways of using up these urges, which we control by mutual agreement and laws. None of these substitute ways, as I suggested before, is perfect, but it is quite possible, within the wide range of behavior allowable in any culture to find ways of behaving sufficiently satisfactorily so that one doesn't get into trouble either with the laws or with one's own personality. In some cases and in some situations that's rather a narrow pathway; it's like walking a tightrope.

Unfortunately, generally speaking, we do not teach our children effectively how to perform this difficult feat—I mean, how to get along with all these arrangements and still not be in trouble with their own personality or with society. The moral of that is, of course, that we should begin to teach psychology in the first year in school, at about five or six years of age, before their ability to think has been entirely spoiled. Children at that age can learn a great deal of sound psychology. For instance, psychology taught to small children, in terms of: What makes people mad? Why do people throw temper tantrums? Why do people behave in this way or that way?—might be very valuable.

Of course, this could be very disconcerting to a father who habitually throws temper tantrums, if little Johnny, aged seven or eight, takes notes for reporting to the class at school. This is likely to upset the discipline of the family, but it might be a very good thing for the father, because Johnny might eventually lead him into greater insight into his own personality—if Johnny survived.

There are relatively easy ways of using up these tensions and pressures, without getting in trouble with the laws and without damaging one's own personality. All it requires is a dynamic use of imagination.

It might be well, now, to return to that other function of imagination, the role of imagination in exploration. Imagination, as I suggested previously, can be used as a scout or a spy to send out into unknown or partially known territory, in order to explore and to experiment with all kinds of behavior or with all kinds of thinking, without being caught and without being punished; to be able to explore in all fields, independently of the local customs of the natives and the moralities of either our ancestors or our own cultures. Yet if imagination has been crippled, as most of our imaginations have been crippled in some way, blinded in some way, incapable of exploring in some areas, unreliable in the reports that it brings back to us, it follows inevitably that our behavior will not be appropriate to the new circumstances in which we find ourselves. This is the position which most of us are in today, because our imaginations have developed within a culture and within a subculture, and within a family within a subculture, and each of these limitations has done something to our imagination, has set bounds to it, has prescribed directions, has in some way distorted or limited the freedom of our imagination.

We are now under the necessity, the absolute necessity, of functioning as world citizens, as part of the human race. We find, if we think about it, that our locally bred or determined imaginations are not really active enough or reliable enough to be effective on a world stage. This is because the things that our imaginations tell us about other kinds of people and other parts of the world are determined by our own culture, not by what those other people are or by what the other parts of the world are. Our imaginations are dependent, determined by the viewpoint that surrounds us when we are children, when our consciences are being formed, when we are learning just exactly what is good and what is bad, and who the good people are—people like us—and who the bad people are —people who are not like us.

It is rather easy to demonstrate that our imagination suffers from some limitation or at least that we don't very frequently take our imagination out for a real run and let it go freely in all directions. Anything that is taught to us in childhood as absolute has this effect. Anything that we believe is permanent and final and unquestionable has this effect of limiting our imagination throughout the rest of our lives, unless we take very specific and determined measures to try to loosen up this imagination and learn to give it exercise.

Most of us were not taught how to do this. We were taught one attitude, which was good, and by inference (if not specifically) that all other attitudes were bad, and people who have bad attitudes are bad people. We also learned, most of us in our childhood, that bad people should be punished, it's good for them, and enjoyable, apparently, to the people that do the punishing. And so we have felt justified in doing our best to beat other kinds of people out of the way they are and trying to impose our attitudes and our ways on them even when our ways and our attitudes would obviously be unsuitable for them. Much less have we recognized that many of our own attitudes and ways are also unsuitable for us.

It may be useful to try right now a little exercise in imagination. Suppose, for instance, that we live not here in this very secure and pleasant part of the world but in another part of the world—say in Southeast Asia somewhere. The first thing we would feel, if we imagine ourselves born and brought up in that part of the world, is hunger; chronic hunger; hunger about which we in North America know nothing; the kind of hunger that is felt when a person has never in his life had enough to eat to feel satisfied; when almost every person is suffering from malnutrition, plus intercurrent diseases caused by malnutrition.

It is difficult to imagine ourselves hungry in that sense. I don't mean just having come in late from a golf game and being ravenous for one's dinner. I mean a hunger that has never been satisfied, with one's children having swollen bellies because of malnutrition, waking and whining in the night for food that cannot be supplied. This is the primary fact of life for most of the people in the world, and if we place ourselves in their position even briefly, we will get a

different point of view on many things that go on in the
world from that which we are accustomed to seeing from
where we happen to be in North America.

In the first place, we would find that we are somewhat
impatient, that we don't have too much patience with
people who would like to sit down and talk nicely with us
about something that would be useful and helpful after
twenty-five or thirty or fifty years. Hungry people are not
usually patient people, and there is no reason why we
should expect them to be as patient as we can afford to be.

To see things through the eyes of others should be the
normal function of a healthy imagination, so from their eyes
let us look at North America. Although there is no one un-
varying way of seeing it truly from any place, we would
find some attitudes rather common at least. We would certainly find a great envy of the people who live in North
America; also, we would find a somewhat limited gratitude;
that is, a recognition that the people of North America
have been extremely generous. They have given away more
than any people before in human history, but we would
note also that in doing so they haven't really hurt themselves very much. They probably haven't reduced their
standard of living even by 1 percent—perhaps not one
tenth of 1 percent—perhaps less than that. So we can't
give them a great deal of credit for self-sacrifice in giving
this extensive aid that we have enjoyed and are enjoying.
However, we do appreciate their generosity, and we are
grateful, within certain limitations.

We do not particularly admire those people in North
America. We know, as apparently they do not know, that

they are the most wasteful people in the world, that they destroy and throw away more stuff than would keep an equal number of people alive in some other place in the world. We know that we could live in luxury on the garbage dumps of North America—real luxury, from our point of view. We know that those people in North America have destroyed tremendous quantities of food while we were starving. We know that they are now limiting their production of food, reducing it, because we are not able to buy it; we don't have the money for it. We recognize that the people in North America have enormous leisure, that they have no real worries at all, because nobody is hungry, nobody is dying of starvation, nobody is dying of exposure. So it's quite clear that they don't have a single thing in the world to worry about. Therefore they ought to have plenty of time to consider world problems, and we wonder why they don't get around to it when they have all this leisure, physical and emotional, which should be invested in world causes.

We know that they have great thinkers. We know that they have tremendous machines. We know they have more equipment than anybody else in the world, greater resources than anybody else in the world, and we wonder why they don't use all that for world good. Surely they must, in North America, begin to recognize that their security is indivisible from ours in another part of the world. They surely can't continue to believe that they can survive if we die. It's obvious to us that they can't, and that the human race will survive or will die in the near future, and never again can large parts or small parts of the human race survive at the expense of the rest of the world.

We in other parts of the world see these things rather clearly. We wonder why it is that people in North America aren't working at the problems that we see—of overpopulation, of starvation, of lack of facilities for distribution of food on a world basis. We know when the Food and Agriculture Organization of the United Nations tried to set up a world food council, it was the government of the United States that blocked it, as most people in the United States do not know. But we in other parts of the world do know, and we can't understand why.

Our attitude does include admiration on some scores; of technical ability, yes; of personality and character, no, not generally. The evidence we see of what those people are like and what they mean when they say "The American Way of Life," we think we know, because we see it in the movies they send us. These movies are predominantly gangster movies, and this we accept, because we are simple people who believe what we see, as the American way of life, portrayed by the Americans themselves, and distributed on a world basis for the education of people in other parts of the world. We know it is authentic because it has a certificate at the beginning that says "passed by the board of censors of some place or other, America," and so we can count on the fact that this is a true picture of American culture.

I myself have spent many, many hours trying to convince people from Southeast Asia and from other parts of the world that I have never in all the years I have lived in the United States of America had to cower in doorways or flatten myself in gutters to avoid flying bullets from cars roaring up and down the streets with their machine guns blazing, and they don't believe me, because they have seen it in the pictures supplied by the Americans themselves to illustrate their way of life.

Those of us from some other place who recognize the truth about this wonder why Americans allow this to happen, because those films do more harm than a hundred Voices of America could do good. They almost completely, or more than completely, neutralize much of the true educational work that is being done about North America in our part of the world. Yet when we ask why such films are sent to us, there isn't any answer that makes sense. The only answer apparently is to make money, and we just cannot be convinced that the United States needs money so badly that it would blacken its own reputation in the eyes of hundreds of millions of people to earn a few dollars.

We read their stories and see their movies, which magnify the virtues of their great Indian killers, whose only virtue was that they killed large numbers of Indians, Indians who were most wickedly trying to defend their homes and their wives and their children, and their right to their own country. We do admire their ancestors. Their ancestors had the foresight and aggressive drive to go out and grab the world's best space while the grabbing was good and before the world rules got changed, but now they won't let anybody else get theirs. They pen us up and say that nobody is allowed to go across this boundary or that boundary today while still regarding the aggressive behavior as highly virtuous in their own ancestors. This seems inconsistent to us and confuses us, yet when we try to express this confusion they are apt to call us "stupid" or "backward."

Well, so much for some of the points of view that we can find from that part of the world. Now that we have exercised our imaginations to this extent, let us jump farther away still. Let us leave all the little cultures of this world. Let us really get out into outer space somewhere and suppose that we are intelligent beings, and are arriving at this planet to explore it and to find out what we can about it. We are going to turn up some very strange things and we are going to wonder how they can be true.

Being from outer space, we are totally without prejudice in favor of this or that kind of behavior, this or that local attitude, this or that culture. Instead we are using the general measuring stick that the welfare of individuals— that is, of all individuals—is a good thing. We will write "Excellent" on our report if we find that the human race— all of it—is comfortable, well fed, and secure. We will accept this as a simple original premise, and, with only that point of view, look at what we see if we explore Planet Earth.

Well, naturally, the first thing we would do would be to call for a map, because we would like to see what the geographical layout of this planet is, and once we have a map, we recognize what is land and what is water, and what is mountains and rivers, and so on. We recognize the conventional markings on the map. But then we find a whole set of other markings the like of which we have never seen before and which we can't understand. We ask the planet's inhabitants what they are, and they answer, "Oh, those are the international boundary lines."

We say, "Well, what is that?"

We are told, "Those are just lines between countries. People of one country live on one side and people of another country live on the other."

"But," we ask, "is this a good thing? Should people be kept apart from each other?"

"Of course, they should be kept apart from each other," the earth men would answer. "That's exactly what international boundaries are for. We have more space and better land than some other people. There are countries who do not have enough space for their people or enough land to grow the food to feed them. If we didn't have international boundaries, they might come over to our side of the line and we would have to share what we have. We wouldn't have so much land or space for ourselves anymore."

We could admit the logic of this last statement, from an entirely selfish point of view, but there are still some things we cannot understand. "But how did these things come to be the way they are? Why are these boundaries in the places where they are? Why do some of your inhabitants have more land and space than others? Is it sound for an international boundary to cut across a fertile valley, to cross a river? Why don't you run it along the tops of mountains at least, if you must have international boundaries?"

"Well, really!" the inhabitants say, with obvious impatience. "It isn't a question of whether they are in the

best place or even in the right place or not. This is just
where they are, that's all."

"Why?"

And then we would get what would be to us amazing
explanations: because sometime, somewhere in the past,
somebody was stronger than somebody else and marched in
and took this much land; because somebody ran out of
food at this point in his advance and dug in at this point;
because one time when there was a war on, in the middle
of a battle it started to rain and both armies stopped here.
And we would be told with great pride:

"This is our national boundary, and rightly so. And for
more than 200 or 300 or 600 years our people have fought
to the death to keep this boundary exactly where it is—
unless, of course, we could extend it farther into the territory of somebody else."

And we would be told further, "It is disloyal—almost
sacrilegious—to question these things. We have known and
believed these things since we were children. They are the
way they are, and that's the way we want them."

As visitors from outer space we would come to the inevitable conclusion that loyalties inculcated in childhood
mean limitations on capacity to think for the rest of one's
life, and we would consider this gravely serious. We would
be appalled that the earth's inhabitants did no thinking at
all in these tabooed areas and it would seem to us that
these things vitally needed some thinking about. If we regarded ourselves as some kind of interplanetary judiciary
committee, we might decide that the best solution for the

problems of the human race would be to wipe that race out entirely.

This would be rather a dreadful thing to say to the peoples of the world, apart from the threat of extermination. They would have to picture themselves as being in a common boat; they would have to accept their membership in the human race without limitations to membership in a group, and this is quite outside the bounds of early training and early belief.

Yet if the human race is going to survive into the distant future, we are going to have to develop in that direction. No one can think clearly about the future of mankind without recognizing that some kind of world organization, some kind of world government or confederation is both inevitable and desirable. Security cannot be limited to this group or that, because security for the human race is now, for the first time in human history, indivisible and will always be indivisible in the future.

Bei Fragen zur Produktsicherheit wenden Sie sich bitte an:
If you have any questions regarding product safety,
please contact:

Walter de Gruyter GmbH
Genthiner Straße 13
10785 Berlin
productsafety@degruyterbrill.com